I0017087

JR secLAB

10 Ways to Hack a Web App
CISSP-ISSAP

Learn why and how to build Java web apps secured from the most common security hacks.

Why Worry?
Recent headlines

- Net worm using Google to spread
  - "…uses a flaw in the widely used community forum software known as the PHP Bulletin Board (phpBB) to spread…"

- California reports massive data breach
  - "…The compromised system had the names, addresses, phone numbers, social security numbers, and dates of birth of everyone who provided or received care."

- Google bug exposes e-mail to hackers
  - "…By altering the "From" address field of an e-mail sent to the service, hackers could potentially find out a user's personal information, including passwords. …"

- truckstop.com web application stolen by competitor
  - "…Getloaded's officers also hacked into the code Creative used to operate its website."

Goal

Learn why and how to build Java web apps secured from the most common security hacks

Agenda

- Intro and Overview
  - How vulnerable are web apps?
  - Basics of web hacking
- Web Architecture and Principles
  - How are most web-based Java apps deployed?
- Principles of Secure Programming
  - A "security mantra" for web developers
- 9 Most Common Web Vulnerabilities
  - …and how to fix them in Java

95% of Web Apps Have Vulnerabilities

- Cross-site scripting (80 percent)
- SQL injection (62 percent)
- Parameter tampering (60 percent)
- Cookie poisoning (37 percent)
- Database server (33 percent)
- Web server (23 percent)
- Buffer overflow (19 percent)

Web Attack

- Discover
  - Examine the environment
    - Identify open ports
    - Discover types/versions of apps running
      - Banner grabbing
      - Extensions (.jhtml, .jsp, etc.) and directory structures
  - Generate and examine errors
    - Submit ridiculous input to provoke errors (fuzzing)
    - Database errors, stack traces very helpful
  - Find info left behind (source code, comments, hidden fields)

- Target
  - Login mechanism
  - Input fields
  - Session mgmt
  - Infrastructure

A Word of Warning

- These tools and techniques can be dangerous
- The difference between a hacker and a cracker is…permission
- Admins will see strange activity in logs, and come looking for you
- Authorities are prosecuting even the "good guys" for using these tools

Security Principles of Web Architecture

- Practice defense-in-depth
- Separate services
    - Web server, app server, db server on separate hosts
- Limit privileges of application user
    - File system (chroot or limit privs to read-only)
    - Database system (limit privileges on tables, schemas, etc.)
    - Privileges of running user (xxtomcat, apache, kobayashi, etc.)
- Hide secrets
    - Database account passwords
    - Encryption keys
- Use standard, vetted components, libraries
    - Keep them patched
- Log, and watch logs for unusual activity
- Load-test and tune accordingly

Principles for Secure Coding

- Don't trust input from user
- Review for logic holes
- Leverage vetted resources
  - Infrastructure
  - Components
- Only give information needed
- Build/test to withstand load
  - Expected load
  - Potential DOS attack

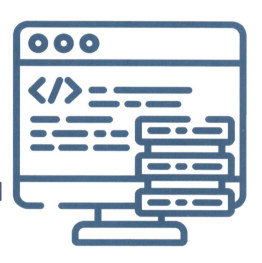

OWASP Top 10 Web Security Vulns

1. Unvalidated input
2. Broken access control
3. Broken account/session management
4. Cross-site scripting (XSS) flaws
5. Buffer overflows
6. Injection flaws
7. Improper error handling
8. Insecure storage
9. Denial-of-service
10. Insecure configuration management

#1: Unvalidated Input

- Attacker can easily change any part of the HTTP request before submitting
  - URL
  - Cookies
  - Form fields
  - Hidden fields
  - Headers

- Input must be validated on the server

- Countermeasures
  - Code reviews (check variable against list of allowed values, not vice-versa)
  - Don't accept unnecessary input from user
  - Store in session or trusted back-end store
  - Sanitize input with regex

What's Wrong With This Picture?

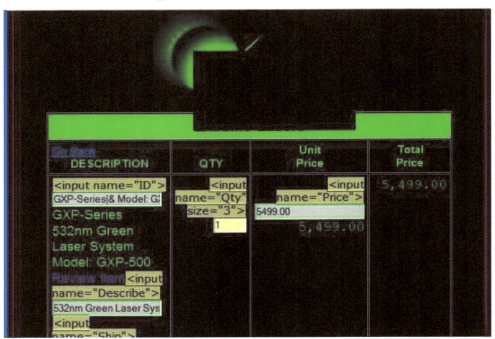

#1: Unvalidated Input (Example)

```java
public void doPost(HttpServletRequest req,…) {
    String customerId =
        req.getParameter("customerId");
    String sku = req.getParameter("sku")
    String stringPrice =
req.getParameter("price")
    Integer price = Integer.valueOf(stringPrice);
    // Store in the database

orderManager.submitOrder(sku,customerId,price);
} // end doPost
```

#1: Unvalidated Input (Corrected)

```java
public void doPost(HttpServletRequest req,…) {
   // Get customer data
   String customerId =
      req.getParameter("customerId");
   String sku = req.getParameter("sku");
   // Get price from database
   Integer price = skuManager.getPrice(sku);
   // Store in the database

orderManager.submitOrder(sku,customerId,price);
} // end doPost
```

#2: Broken Access Control

- Inconsistently applied file system, URL controls
- Examples
  - Path traversal
    - Forced browsing past access control checks
    - File permissions—may allow access to config/password files
  - Logic flaws
  - Client-side caching

- Countermeasures
  - Use non-programmatic controls
  - Access control via central container
  - Code reviews

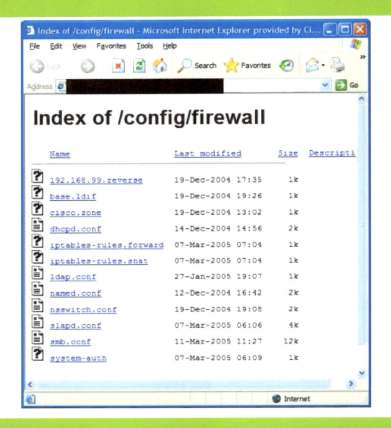

#2: Broken Access Control (Example)

```java
protected void doPost(HttpServletRequest req, HttpServletResponse res) {
    try {
        String username = req.getParameter("USERNAME");
        String password = req.getParameter("PASSWORD");
        try {
            Connection connection = DatabaseUtilities.makeConnection();
            PreparedStatement statement = connection.prepareStatement
                ("SELECT * FROM user_system_data WHERE user_name = ? AND password = ?");
            statement.setString(1,username);
            statement.setString(2,password);
            ResultSet results = statement.executeQuery(query);
            results.first();
            if (results.getString(1).equals("")) {
                s.setMessage("Invalid username and password entered.");
                return (makeLogin(s));
            } // end results check
        } catch (Exception e) {}
        // continue and display the page
        if (username != null && username.length() > 0) {
            return (makeUser(s, username, "PARAMETERS"));
        } // end username test
    } catch (Exception e) {
        s.setMessage("Error generating " + this.getClass().getName());
    } // end try/catch
    return (makeLogin(s));
} // end doPost
```

#2: Broken Access Control (Solution) How to Set Up Basic Authentication

web.xml file

```xml
<security-constraint>
  <web-resource-collection>
      <web-resource-name>Admin</web-resource-name>
      <url-pattern>/jsp/admin/*</url-pattern>
  </web-resource-collection>
  <auth-constraint>
    <role-name>(accessLevel=Admin)</role-name>
  </auth-constraint>
</security-constraint>
<login-config>
  <auth-method>BASIC</auth-method>
  <realm-name>CCO</realm-name>
</login-config>
```

#2: Broken Access Control (Solution) How to Set Up Form Authentication

web.xml file

```xml
<!-- LOGIN AUTHENTICATION -->
  <login-config>
    <auth-method>FORM</auth-method>
    <realm-name>CCO</realm-name>
    <form-login-config>
      <form-login-page>login.jsp</form-login-page>
      <form-error-page>error.jsp</form-error-page>
    </form-login-config>
  </login-config>
```

login.jsp

```html
<form method="POST"  action= "j_security_check" >
 <input type="text"  name= "j_username" >
 <input type="password"  name= "j_password" >
</form>
```

#3: Broken Account and Session Management

- Weak user authentication
  - Password-only
  - Easily guessable usernames (admin, etc.)
  - Poorly implemented single sign-on (SSO)
- Weak resource authentication
  - How are database passwords stored?
    - Could it be disclosed via browser?
  - Using IP to authenticate?
    - Can be spoofed
- Countermeasures
  - Use vetted single sign-on and session mgmt solution
  - Netegrity SiteMinder
  - RSA ClearTrust
  - Strong passwords
  - Remove default user names
  - Protect sensitive files

What's Wrong With This Picture?

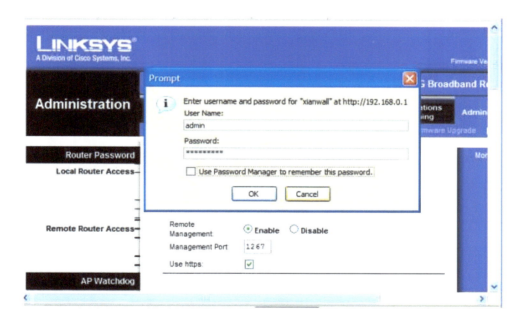

#3: Broken Account/Session Management (Client Example—SSO)

```java
public void doGet(HttpServletRequest req,…) {
    // Get user name
    String userId = req.getRemoteUser();
    Cookie ssoCookie = new Cookie("userid",userId);
    ssoCookie.setPath("/");
    ssoCookie.setDomain("cisco.com");
    response.addCookie(ssoCookie);
    …
}
```

#3: Broken Account/Session Management (Server Example—SSO)

```java
public void doGet(HttpServletRequest req,…) {
    // Get user name
    Cookie[] cookies = req.Cookies();
    for (i=0; i < cookies.length; i++) {
        Cookie cookie = cookies[i];
        if (cookie.getName().equals("ssoCookie")) {
            String userId = cookie.getValue();
            HttpSession session = req.getSession();
            session.setAttribute("userId",userId);
        } // end if
    } // end for
} // end doGet
```

#3: Broken Account/Session Management (Client Solution—SSO)

```
public void doGet(HttpServletRequest req,…) {
  // Get user name
  String userId = req.getRemoteUser();
  encryptedUserId = Encrypter.encrypt(userId);
  Cookie ssoCookie =
    new Cookie("userid",encrypteduserId);
  ssoCookie.setPath("/");
  ssoCookie.setDomain("cisco.com");
  response.addCookie(ssoCookie);
  …
}
```

#3: Broken Account/Session Management (Server Solution—SSO)

```java
public void doGet(HttpServletRequest req,…) {
  // Get user name
  Cookie[] cookies = req.Cookies();
  for (i=0; i < cookies.length; i++) {
    Cookie cookie = cookies[i];
    if (cookie.getName().equals("ssoCookie")) {
        String encryptedUserId = cookie.getValue();
        String userId = Encrypter.decrypt(encryptedUserId);
        if (isValid(userId)) {
            HttpSession session = req.getSession();
            session.setAttribute("userId",userId);
        } // end if isValid…
    } // end if cookie = ssoCookie…
  } // end for
} // end doGet
```

#4: Cross-Site Scripting (XSS)

- Attacker…
    - Inject code into web page that is then displayed to user in the browser
    - Uses trusted application/company to reflect malicious code to end-user
    - Can "hide" the malicious code w/unicode

- Vulnerable anywhere user-supplied data is redisplayed w/out input validation or output encoding

- 2 types of attacks: stored and reflected

- Can steal cookies, especially vulnerable on apps with form-based authentication

- Countermeasures
    - Input validation
        - White-listing: a-z, A-Z, 0-9, etc.)
        - Black-listing: "< > ( ) # &"
        - Don't forget these: "&lt &gt &#40 &#41 &#35 &#38"
    - Output encoding (htmlEncode output)
    - Truncate input fields to reasonable length

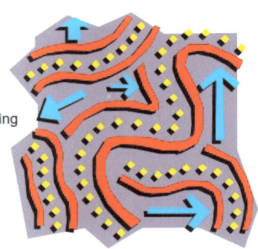

What's Wrong With This Picture?

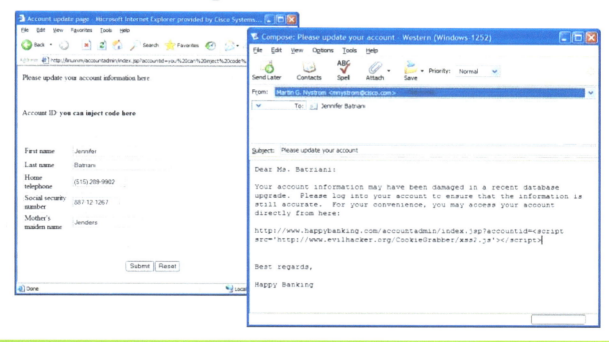

#4: Cross-Site Scripting (Flaw)

```java
protected void doPost(HttpServletRequest req, HttpServletResponse res) {

    String title = req.getParameter("TITLE");

    String message = req.getParameter("MESSAGE");

  try {

      connection = DatabaseUtilities.makeConnection(s);

      PreparedStatement statement =
        connection.prepareStatement
          ("INSERT INTO messages VALUES(?,?)");

      statement.setString(1,title);

      statement.setString(2,message);

      statement.executeUpdate();

    } catch (Exception e) {

      …

    } // end catch

} // end doPost
```

#4: Cross-Site Scripting (Solution)

```java
private static String stripEvilChars(String evilInput) {

    Pattern evilChars = Pattern.compile("[^a-zA-Z0-9]");

    return evilChars.matcher(evilInput).replaceAll("");

}

protected void doPost(HttpServletRequest req, HttpServletResponse res) {

  String title = stripEvilChars(req.getParameter("TITLE"));

  String message = stripEvilChars(req.getParameter("MESSAGE"));

  try {

      connection = DatabaseUtilities.makeConnection(s);

      PreparedStatement statement =

        connection.prepareStatement

            ("INSERT INTO messages VALUES(?,?)");

      statement.setString(1,title);

      statement.setString(2,message);

      statement.executeUpdate();

    } catch (Exception e) {

      ...

    } // end catch

} // end doPost
```

#5: Buffer Overflow Errors

- Not generally an issue with Java apps
- Avoid use of native methods
  - Especially from untrusted sources

#6: Injection Flaws

- Allows attacker to relay malicious code in form variables or URL
  - System commands
  - SQL
- Typical dangers
  - Runtime.exec() to external programs (like sendmail)
  - Dynamically concatenated SQL statements
- Examples
  - Path traversal: "../"
  - Add more commands: "; rm –r *"
  - SQL injection: "' OR 1=1"
- Countermeasures
  - Use PreparedStatements in SQL
  - Avoid Runtime.exec() calls (use libraries instead)
  - Run with limited privileges
  - Filter/validate input

What's Wrong With This Picture?

Enter an Account Number: `101' OR 1=1` [Go!]

userid	first_name	last_name	cc_number	cc_type
101	Joe	Blow	987654321	VISA
101	Joe	Blow	222200001111	MC
102	John	Doe	222200002222	MC
102	John	Doe	222200002222	AMEX
103	Jane	Plane	123456789	MC
103	Jane	Plane	333300003333	AMEX

#6: SQL Injection (Flaw)

```java
protected void doPost(HttpServletRequest req, HttpServletResponse res) {
    String query =
      "SELECT userid, name FROM user_data WHERE accountnum = '"
      + req.getParameter("ACCT_NUM")
      + "'";
    PrintWriter out = res.getWriter();
    // HTML stuff to out.println...
    try {
      connection = DatabaseUtilities.makeConnection(s);
      Statement statement = connection.createStatement();
      ResultSet results = statement.executeQuery(query);
      while (results.next ()) {
         out.println("<TR><TD>" + rset.getString(1) + "</TD>")
         out.println("<TD>" + rset.getString(2) + "</TD>")
      } // end while
    } catch (Exception e) {
      // exception handling...
    } // end catch
} // end doPost
```

```java
protected void doPost(HttpServletRequest req, HttpServletResponse res) {
    PrintWriter out = res.getWriter();
    // HTML stuff to out.println...
    try {
        connection = DatabaseUtilities.makeConnection(s);
        PreparedStatement statement = connection.prepareStatement
            ("SELECT userid, name FROM user_data WHERE accountnum = ?");
        statement.setString(1,req.getParameter("ACCT_NUM"));
        ResultSet results = statement.executeQuery(query);
        while (results.next()) {
            out.println("<TR><TD>" + rset.getString(1) + "</TD>");
            out.println("<TD>" + rset.getString(2) + "</TD>");
        } // end while
    } catch (Exception e) {
      // exception handling...
    } // end catch
} // end doPost
```

#7: Improper Error Handling

- Examples: stack traces, DB dumps
- Helps attacker know how to target the app
- Often left behind during programmer debugging
- Inconsistencies can be revealing
  - "File not found" vs. "Access denied"

- Gives insight into source code
  - Logic flaws
  - Default accounts, etc.
- Good messages give enough info to user w/o giving too much info to attacker
- Countermeasures
  - Code review
  - Modify default error pages (404, 401, etc.)
  - Log details to log files, not returned in HTTP request

What's Wrong With This Picture?

General Error

Could not obtain post/user information.

DEBUG MODE

SQL Error : 1016 Can't open file: 'nuke_bbposts_text.MYD'. (errno: 145)

SELECT u.username, u.user_id, u.user_posts, u.user_from, u.user_website, u.user_email, u.user_icq, u.user_aim, u.user_yim, u.user_regdate, u.user_msnm, u.user_viewemail, u.user_rank, u.user_sig, u.user_sig_bbcode_uid, u.user_avatar, u.user_avatar_type, u.user_allowavatar, u.user_allowsmile, p.*, pt.post_text, pt.post_subject, pt.bbcode_uid FROM nuke_bbposts p, nuke_users u, nuke_bbposts_text pt WHERE p.topic_id = '1547' AND pt.post_id = p.post_id AND u.user_id = p.poster_id ORDER BY p.post_time ASC LIMIT 0, 15

Line : 435
File : /usr/home/geeks/www/vonage/modules/Forums/viewtopic.php

#7: Improper Error Handling (Flaw)

```java
protected void doPost(HttpServletRequest req, HttpServletResponse res) {
    String query =
      "SELECT userid, name FROM user_data WHERE accountnum = '"
      + req.getParameter("ACCT_NUM") + "'";
    PrintWriter out = res.getWriter();
    // HTML stuff to out.println...
    try {
      connection = DatabaseUtilities.makeConnection(s);
      Statement statement = connection.createStatement();
      ResultSet results = statement.executeQuery(query);
      while (results.next()) {
        out.println("<TR><TD>" + rset.getString(1) + "</TD>")
        out.println("<TD>" + rset.getString(2) + "</TD>")
      } // end while
    } catch (Exception e) {
      e.printStackTrace(out);
    } // end catch
} // end doPost
```

#7: Improper Error Handling (Solution)

```java
protected void doPost HttpServletRequest req, HttpServletResponse res) {
    String query =
      "SELECT userid, name FROM user_data WHERE accountnum = '"
      + req.getParameter("ACCT_NUM") + "'";
    PrintWriter out = res.getWriter();
    // HTML stuff to out.println_
    try {
      connection = DatabaseUtilities.makeConnection(s);
      Statement statement = connection.createStatement();
      ResultSet results = statement.executeQuery query);
      while (results.next ()) {
      out.println("<TR><TD>" + rset.getString(1) + "</TD>");
      out.println("<TD>" + rset.getString(2) + "</TD>");
      } // end while
  } catch  Exception e) {
      Logger logger = Logger.getLogger();
      logger.log(Level.SEVERE "Error retrieving account number",e);
      out.println("Sorry, but we are unable to retrieve this account");
    } // end catch
} // end doPost
```

#8: Insecure Storage

- Sensitive data such as credit cards, passwords, etc. must be protected
- Examples of bad crypto
  - Poor choice of algorithm
  - Poor randomness in sessions/tokens
- Storage locations must be protected
  - Database
  - Files
  - Memory
- Countermeasures
  - Store only what you must
  - Store a hash instead of the full value if you can (SHA-1, for example)
  - Use only vetted, public cryptography

Encoding Is Not Encrypting

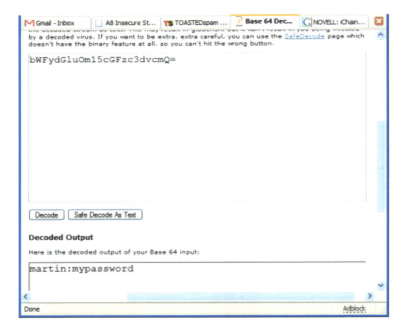

#8: Insecure Storage—Bad Example

```java
public String encrypt(String plainText) {
  plainText = plainText.replace("a", "z");
  plainText = plainText.replace("b", "y");
  …
  return Base64Encoder.encode(plainText);
}
```

#8: Insecure Storage—Fixed Example

```java
public String encrypt(String plainText) {
    // Read encryptKey as a byte array from a file
    DESKeySpec keySpec = new DESKeySpec(encryptKey);
    SecretKeyFactory factory =
        new SecretKeyFactory.getInstance("DES");
    SecretKey key = factory.generateSecret(keySpec);
    Cipher cipher = Cipher.getInstance("DES");
    cipher.init(Cipher.ENCRYPT_MODE,key);
    byte[] utf8text = plainText.getBytes("UTF8");
    byte[] enryptedText = ecipher.doFinal(utf8text);
    return Base64Encoder.encode(encryptedText);
}
```

#9: Denial-Of-Service (DoS)

- Examples that may provoke DoS
  - Heavy object allocation/reclamation
  - Overuse of logging
  - Unhandled exceptions
  - Unresolved dependencies on other systems
    - Web services
    - Databases
- May impact other applications, hosts, databases, or network itself
- Countermeasures
  - Load testing
  - Code review

#10: Insecure Configuration Management

- Tension between "work out of the box" and "use only what you need"

- Developers ? web masters

- Examples
  - Unpatched security flaws (BID example)
  - Misconfigurations that allow directory traversal
  - Administrative services accessible
  - Default accounts/passwords

- Countermeasures
  - Create and use hardening guides
  - Turn off all unused services
  - Set up and audit roles, permissions, and accounts
  - Set up logging and alerts

Review: Principles for Secure Coding

- Don't trust input from user
- Watch for logic holes
- Leverage common, vetted resources
- Only give information needed
- Leverage vetted infrastructure and components
- Build/test to withstand load
  - Expected load
  - Potential DOS attack

For More Information

- References
  - *Top 10 Web Application Vulnerabilities* (OWASP)
  - *Innocent Code*, by Sverre H. Huseby
- Tools used in this preso
- WebGoat—vulnerable web applications for demonstration
- VMWare—runs Linux and Windows 2000 virtual machines on demo laptop
- nmap—host/port scanning to find vulnerable hosts
- Mozilla Firefox—browser that supports plug-ins for proxied HTTP, source browsing
  - SwitchProxy plug-in lets you quickly switch your proxies
  - WebDeveloper plug-in lets you easily clear HTTP auth
- WebScarab—HTTP proxy

Q&A

JR secLAB

10 Ways to Hack a Web App
CISSP-ISSAP

Learn why and how to build Java web apps secured from the most common security hacks.

www.ingramcontent.com/pod-product-compliance
Lightning Source LLC
LaVergne TN
LVHW060202050326
832903LV00016B/344